THEN & NOW

NOVATO

From 1956 to 1977, Novatans celebrated the Western Weekend and Rodeo, which was cosponsored by the Junior Chamber and the Novato Horsemen. This event was an outgrowth of a parade and horse show organized by the Novato Horsemen in 1945; by the 1960s, more than 20,000 people lined the streets to watch the annual parade. In this photograph from the late 1950s, Walter Antonio Sr. leads a goat cart with Jeanie and Bonnie Antonio on board. (Courtesy of the Novato History Museum.)

NOVATO

Novato Historical Guild
with Ron Vela

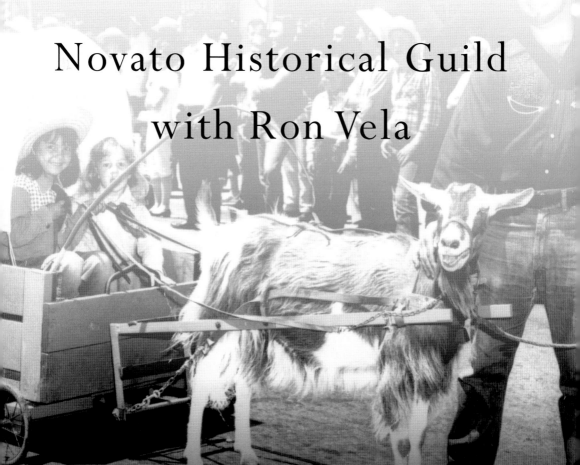

For the volunteers of the Novato History Museum and Archives and the donors of historic images to its collections, we are grateful for your dedication to preserving local history.

Copyright © 2009 by Novato Historical Guild with Ron Vela
ISBN 978-0-7385-7194-2

Library of Congress Control Number: 2009929057

Published by Arcadia Publishing
Charleston SC, Chicago IL, Portsmouth NH, San Francisco CA

Printed in the United States of America

For all general information contact Arcadia Publishing at:
Telephone 843-853-2070
Fax 843-853-0044
E-mail sales@arcadiapublishing.com
For customer service and orders:
Toll-Free 1-888-313-2665

Visit us on the Internet at www.arcadiapublishing.com

ON THE FRONT COVER: The Novato History Museum, located in the oldest house in Novato, overlooks the newest construction in downtown, a Whole Foods grocery store and the Millworks apartments. Grant Avenue is the main street in both pictures. During the 50-year span between the two photographs, many of the old buildings are still visible, but many open spaces have been filled in with buildings. The eastern end of Grant Avenue was anchored by the railroad, and the western end fanned out to orchards and dairies. Now most of the land is commercial and residential property. (Then image courtesy of Novato History Museum, now image courtesy of Ron Vela.)

ON THE BACK COVER: Grant Avenue around 1914 shows what many would consider the quintessential western town: cowboys herded cattle down the dirt street, and the road was lined with wooden sidewalks and horse troughs. (Courtesy of the Novato History Museum.)

CONTENTS

Acknowledgments   vii
Introduction   ix

1.   Grant Avenue   11

2.   Ranches and Farms   35

3.   Residences   47

4.   Points of Interest   59

5.   Community Life   69

6.   Civic Life   83

ACKNOWLEDGMENTS

Since its inception in 1976, the Novato Historical Guild has had so many volunteers contribute their time and skills to keep Novato's history alive that it would be impossible to thank everyone who has had a role in preserving our local history. The Novato Historical Guild, in cooperation with the City of Novato, operates the Novato History Museum. Unless otherwise noted, all historical images in this book are from the collection of the Novato History Museum, and all modern photographs are by Ron Vela.

Novato Historical Guild members formed an author team to complete this book. Kay Antongiovanni, Janice Bazurto, Diana Goebel, Kathryn Keena Hansen, Dorothy Hicks, Yvette Jackson, Sheryl Jones, Anne Lehan, Edna Angel Manzoni, Jim McNern, Cynthia Nunes Motsinger, Michael Read, Stephen Schwindt, John Trumbull, Susan Trumbull, Ron Vela, William Wright, Iva Young, and museum curator Samantha Kimpel contributed research, chose images, and wrote and edited text. Ron Vela climbed hills, drove back roads, and made a lot of new friends in town as he completed all the modern-day photography in the book.

We would not have been able to produce the book as easily without May Rodgers Ungemach's book *Novato Township*. This book continues to be an invaluable resource for the guild and museum. We would like to thank the volunteers, interns, and collections assistants who work to make the archives and collections the wonderful resource that they are: Anna Morrison, Ann Ramsay, Marie Salmina, Bill Almeida, Eva Slott, Judy Walker, James McCabe, Brittany Spencer, and Philip Lehman-Brown.

And finally, we want to extend special thanks to the past and present board of directors of the Novato Historical Guild for their support of this project as well as for their exemplary support for the Novato History Museum.

INTRODUCTION

With its gentle climate and rolling hills, Novato, California, has long been recognized for its beauty and agricultural potential. Modern history stems from a Mexican land grant known as the Rancho de Novato, which was purchased by Joseph Sweetser and Francis DeLong in 1856. They planted thousands of fruit trees, and soon Novato blossomed into one of the largest apple orchards in the world.

The arrival of Portuguese and Swiss-Italian farmers and dairymen in the 1870s helped to further establish the town as an agricultural center, and the arrival of Northwestern Pacific Railroad 10 years later helped connect the growing town with the rest of the San Francisco Bay. Novato became a vital center of food production for the entire bay area, as vineyards, dairies, orchards, and ranches formed the base of the local economy. DeLong's 6,000 acres, purchased and subdivided by the Home and Farm Company in 1888, formed the beginning of what is now the City of Novato, which was incorporated in 1960.

Although now a city of 50,000, as a result of the city's relatively low population density, Novato continues to possess a small-town, rural atmosphere. Nearby hills, lakes, and scenic back roads offer visitors and residents numerous opportunities for recreation and adventure. The city contains over 3,000 acres of preserves, open spaces, and 27 city parks.

Many of Novato's pioneer families still live in the town—the names of their forebears are preserved as street names, regions, and landmarks and documented in the archives of the Novato History Museum. Their recollections form a vital link between present and past. This is the basis by which the present community orients itself in time.

Among the most precious of the city's resources is its history, documented in the landscape and artifacts left by those who have lived here before and kept alive in the collective memory of those who continue to call this place home.

As Novato celebrates the 50th anniversary of its incorporation, great changes are underway. Passenger trains will once again be rolling through the city after nearly half a century, city government will be returning to a newly restored city hall, and ambitious developments are taking root in the heart of downtown. For some, these changes are a hopeful sign of return to better days. For others, their pace and scale is out of character with the rhythm of the community. But for everyone, the changing landscape affords an opportunity to reconsider the connection to the past and, perhaps more important, to the future.

GRANT AVENUE

NOVATO CAL.

Grant Avenue—Novato's "Main Street"—developed as a result of the establishment of the train depot in the 1880s. This photograph was taken in 1914 looking west from above Railroad Avenue. What is now city hall can be seen at the left, and Grant Avenue can be seen running up slightly right of center. Druids Hall, at the corner of Grant Avenue and Reichert Avenue, is seen at the center. Grant Avenue is the heart of present-day Novato's Old Town and is a thriving, revitalized retail and restaurant destination. This chapter begins with the street's beginnings at Railroad Avenue and progresses to where it ends on Novato Boulevard.

Swiss immigrant Abraham Yelmorini settled in Novato in 1900. He and his family operated a saloon on the ground floor of their home across from the train station. Local lore is that he built the Flat Iron Building (1908) so that passengers getting off the train would not be able to see the other saloons on Grant Avenue and would patronize his business instead. There have been many tenants in the building over the years; it is currently occupied by Morris and Company, a home accessories retail store.

The Novato House Hotel, built by the Home and Farm Company in the 1880s, was Novato's leading hotel. After retiring as a schooner pilot, Capt. Leon Hiribarren purchased the business in 1899, and his family managed the hotel, saloon, and livery stable. The present building was constructed in 1954–1955 by Jim Brashear and opened as Jim's Sport Shop. It had several owners before closing in the 1970s and opening again as Marin Color II.

E. R. Samuels operated his store at 750 Grant Avenue in the 1920s and 1930s. An active citizen, he also served a term as a Marin County supervisor and coached Novato's first semipro baseball team, the Novato Colts, in addition to his duties as the store owner. A two-story professional office building is now on the site, and the Grant Avenue side of the first floor has sheltered a succession of upscale restaurants.

Stephen Porcella's Fashion Shop at 800 Grant Avenue was built around 1893. Ranchers from all over Marin County came to have Porcella make and repair their iron equipment. Porcella also built wagons, filed saws for carpenters, and filled many special orders. In the old photograph, Stephen Porcella is on the right and Sandy McIntosh is on the left; they worked together until 1939, and McIntosh retired in 1950. Today the popular coffee shop and café Dr. Insomnia occupies this building.

Guglielmo and Natalina Torassa built the Torassa Building in 1937. Guglielmo Torassa was a baker in his native Italy, and he and his wife owned and operated the Torassa Bakery in the adjacent building (see page 72). In 1945, when the Novato branch of the Marin County Library needed more space, it was moved to the ground floor of the Torassa Building, where it remained until a permanent home was built on Novato Boulevard in the 1960s. For the past 23 years, Alice Becker has operated a women's clothing store in the site of the former library space.

By 1914, the "new" town of Novato was becoming well established around the train depot. John Teixeira Verissimo built the Verissimo Building on Grant Avenue next to Loustanau Hall (now Druids Hall). The building contained three storefronts with a small house in the rear where the family lived. Today the structure houses Masa's Japanese Restaurant, a popular spot since 1990, and Anokha, Cuisine of India. The building was remodeled in 2009.

This building, located at 815–817 Grant Avenue, was built in 1910 to expand the hardware business Charles Edgar Carlile originally started in the Flat Iron Building. The hardware store was known for the range of items that were considered "hard to find." Following Carlile's death in 1961, the site has been home to many businesses. Today a women's contemporary clothing store occupies the site.

Fred S. Hamilton came to Novato from Kansas in 1904. He operated a general store on the southeast corner of Grant Avenue and Sherman Street until 1917. His home was located directly behind the store at 820 Sherman Avenue. The modern building that now occupies the site houses professional offices on the second floor (Martha Thorup, CPA) and Grazie, an Italian restaurant, on the street level.

In 1913, James Black Burdell financed Novato's first bank and became its first president. The Novato Bank was constructed at 826 Grant Avenue by Frank Silva, who owned the property. The adjoining building to the west was a drugstore for a few years, and from 1917 to 1951, the U.S. Post Office occupied that site. Today the old bank building is a retail site, New Shoes for Kids. The other stores that currently serve Novato on this site are a gallery in the old post office and boutiques, a bakery, and a tailor in the adjacent building that served at one point as H. Pini and Company.

Scott's General Store was built by A. D. Scott in 1890. The ground floor housed the store, while the second floor, with its large open room, provided space for plays, meetings, and religious services. A furniture store once occupied both up and downstairs, and in recent years, the downstairs has served as home to a music store, a western wear and supplies store, several boutiques, and a beauty store. For 25 years, Dennis Hagerty's State Farm Insurance offices have been located on the second floor.

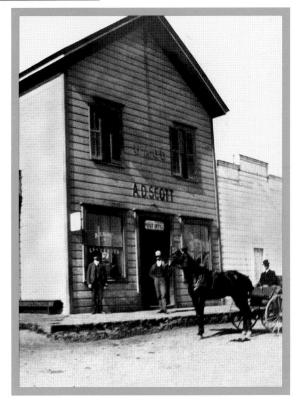

A panorama of Grant Avenue from around 1914 shows what many would consider the quintessential western town: cowboys herded cattle down the dirt street, and the road was lined with wooden sidewalks and horse troughs. In the early 2000s, the City of Novato spent $11 million to revitalize the downtown corridor and installed a new street, sidewalks, and trees. As seen in the comparison between then and now, the street retains much of its original scale and historic charm.

On July 1, 1922, the first copy of the *Novato Advance* was printed in the Flat Iron Building (see page 12). Within a year, the paper moved to a new location at 868 Grant Avenue. Editor William Hanen planned to publish a monthly newspaper. However, the response to the paper was so enthusiastic that by September 1924, the paper became a weekly, which it remains to this day. The paper has moved to other buildings in downtown through the years, and this building has been used for restaurants in recent years; it is currently occupied by the Italian restaurant Portelli.

Tom Sutton ran one of several livery stables in Novato near the dawn of the 20th century. Sutton, seen below, was "roadmaster" for the valley, in charge of collecting road maintenance taxes, in addition to being the constable for the area. The Quonset hut structure now on the site was erected in the mid-20th century. It has been Old Town Sports, a sporting goods store at 817 Grant Avenue, since the 1960s, specializing in bicycling and skiing equipment.

The Novato Theater is located on the site of the second H. Pini and Company, which burned in 1945. The theater was constructed and operated by Alfred Bowman. In May 1947, the first film shown was *The Al Jolson Story*. The last film was shown in the 1990s, and the theater is currently vacant. The building is a prominent site on Grant Avenue in an area that is being revitalized and maintained historically.

The Novato Pharmacy was owned by Bill Nave and Paul Elmore, and the pharmacist was Lee Johnson. Johnson's wife ran the soda fountain, which was a popular gathering place for coffee and conversation, as well as for Novato Grammar School students from across the street. Upon the death of Lee Johnson, Nave and Elmore sold the business to Ralph Kemerer in 1949. In 1956, the pharmacy moved to 1416 Grant Avenue. Today this corner is the heart of the revitalized downtown commercial district.

Novato Grammar School (also known as Grant Avenue School) was the third school built in Novato. It was dedicated on June 15, 1922, and Lulu Sutton was the principal. After it was no longer used as a school, the Church of Jesus Christ of Latter-day Saints leased it for several years. The building was demolished in 1959 since it did not meet earthquake standards. Today McDonald's restaurant is in the vicinity of where the school stood. The Novato Police Department is approximately where the upper playground existed.

Louis J. Nave opened his garage on the corner of Grant Avenue and Redwood Highway (Redwood Boulevard) around 1915. He sold new cars and repaired the ailing ones. At mid-century, a second floor was added that contains four apartments. Various businesses have occupied the ground floor, including a drugstore (see page 26), a deli, barbershops, a pet store, a feed store, and a bakery. Marin Trophies has occupied the corner since 1975, as well as Lee's Barber Shop and Old Town Artworks.

ON THE RED-WOOD HIGHWAY
NOVATO. CAL.
DECKER STUDIO

Rodoni's Richfield Service Station was in a prime location on the southwest corner of old Highway 101 (now Redwood Boulevard) and Grant Avenue. This vintage photograph was taken in the early 1950s and shows, from left to right, Jackie Smith and Manuel Pimentel, manager. In those days, service was included: gas was pumped, all of the windows were washed, oil and tire pressure was checked, and gas was about 25¢ per gallon. Today WestAmerica Bank occupies the site.

At the intersection of Redwood Boulevard (then Highway 101) and Grant Avenue on the northwest corner was DeBorba's Stage Station, a favorite stopping place during the early to mid-1900s for motorists returning from Russian River recreational spots. The structure was originally built as a real estate office for John Sweetser in 1913–1914, when he began subdividing and selling land west of the highway. When the highway was widened in 1945–1946, the building was moved to another site (see page 64). The site is now occupied by a commercial building that currently houses a day spa/salon.

Prior to World War II, Novato's downtown was located mainly between the State Highway (Redwood Boulevard) and Railroad Avenue. For the most part, West Grant Avenue consisted of scattered homes and dairies. By 1947, the town was developing; Gordon Anderson moved his Chevrolet Motor Company to the west side of the State Highway, and Pini Hardware and a drugstore had opened as well. Today Redwood Credit Union replaces Anderson Motor Company, Pini Hardware has moved elsewhere, and a new and improved Grant Avenue welcomes shoppers to the many businesses located there.

This was the second church built by Our Lady of Loretto parish. This building was constructed and dedicated in 1937, after fire destroyed the previous church (see page 88). Architect Henry A. Minton chose the mission-style frame and a stucco exterior. When the parish needed to expand and build a larger church (now at Novato Boulevard and Grant Avenue), the Grant Avenue property was sold to the Picchi family in 1963. Since 1991, the Boje family has operated the Cacti Restaurant.

Novato pioneers Henry and Lorena Manzoni built this home and farm at 1009 Fifth Street in 1916. Henry was hired by Fred Wiley Sweetser to build First through Seventh Streets from Grant Avenue to Vallejo Avenue with a primitive horse-pulled road grader. As Novato's business developed west to Seventh Street, the Manzoni property was sold 1960. Constructed by 1962, the three-story Talbot Building was the first in town to have an elevator (below, left). The fire department purchased a new truck that would allow them to fight a fire on the third level. Currently, a mix of restaurants, retail, and professional offices occupy the building. (Then image courtesy of the Manzoni family.)

One of the many community activities sponsored by the Novato Volunteer Firemen's Association was the annual Easter Egg Hunt. Seen here are children accompanied by their parents in the late 1950s on the vacant property bordered by Virginia Avenue, the end of Grant Avenue, and Novato Boulevard. Every year, about 2,000 eggs were dyed and hidden by the firemen on the Saturday before Easter. Now this formerly vacant lot houses Our Lady of Loretto Catholic Church.

CHAPTER 2

RANCHES AND FARMS

Rancho de Novato, located in northwestern Novato, was purchased by Joseph Bryant Sweetser and Francis DeLong in 1856. They planted fruit trees and vineyards on the ranch. Their apples were shipped all over the United States and to other countries. At the time, the orchard was considered one of the largest in the world. In 1870, Sweetser sold all but one square mile (which is now downtown Novato west of Redwood Boulevard) to his partner, DeLong. The rancho was subdivided for housing in the mid-20th century.

Ignacio Pacheco discovered the Rancho de San Jose in 1834 and asked to trade it for his Agua Caliente Rancho, which was granted. He first built an adobe home that remained on the property until it burned in 1925. One of his sons, Gumesindo Pacheco, built a large home on the southern portion of the rancho. Herb Rowland Jr., a great-great-grandson of Ignacio Pacheco, now owns the Gumesindo Pacheco Mansion. Rowland is the only original grantee in the state of California still living on his property. The Novato Historical Guild is seen here visiting Rowland's home and winery in 2008.

BAY VIEW, SAN JOSE PACHECO RANCHO.

SAN JOSE PACHECO RANCHO.

The Louis Buzzini ranch, shown above in 1947, included all of the land west of Highway 101 between Novato Creek and Highway 37. Richard Wright Hanna purchased the 1,000-acre parcel of mostly tidal land in 1958 and worked to improve the drainage facilities on the land. Some of the land remains open space, especially adjacent to San Pablo Bay. At the center is the current site of Vintage Oaks at Novato, a 600,000-square-foot shopping plaza that is anchored by superstores such as Target and Costco.

Located on Indian Valley Road and Gage Lane, the 25-acre James Gage Breeding Farm and Hatchery was devoted exclusively to the breeding of single-comb white leghorns. The hatchery was known nationwide and shipped baby chicks all over the country and abroad. More than 4,000 mature breeding hens were constantly mated with males of high pedigree. The ranch was sold in 1941 to Harold Bloom, who operated it as a poultry ranch until his death. The ranch was subdivided into 14 home sites on Bloom Lane.

RANCHES AND FARMS

Christian Hansen, a Danish immigrant, purchased 12 acres, mostly fruit orchards, at Eucalyptus Avenue and Center Road in 1911 from the Novato Land Company. He removed the orchards and turned the property into a successful chicken ranch. It was sold to Otto Gearhardt in 1924, who is seen here feeding his chickens. The area was later subdivided into home sites.

Located on Olive Avenue, the 40-acre Gnoss Ranch was purchased in 1905 for $4,000. The ranch consisted of apple, pear, peach, prune, and apricot orchards. There were also 5,000 laying hens, along with cows and pigs raised on the ranch. The pears were shipped to the San Francisco Farmers' Market and throughout the bay area. Bill Gnoss was the Marin County Fifth District supervisor and an active Novato community leader for many years. His brother, George Gnoss, was Marin County clerk. In 1962, the ranch was sold and subdivided into 91 home sites and is known as Gnoss Estates.

RANCHES AND FARMS

First known as the Clark Ranch, this land was owned by Julia Pacheco Bodkin. She leased the property to David Leveroni and then to William Hale, an Irish immigrant, in 1923. Hale operated a dairy and raised hay and grain as well as a herd of beef cattle. In 1964, the McGraw-Hill Book Company bought 100 acres (a portion of the original ranch) and constructed a book depository. The building later served as a distribution center for Birkenstock USA, but the building is currently vacant. Both the Leveroni and Hale families remain in the dairy and ranching businesses.

Located along Novato Boulevard, the Parkhaven town house development was formerly a cheese factory started by the Novato Land Company in 1898. The 60-acre site known as Oliva Ranch was leased by David Leveroni Sr., who grew grapes and hay. It was later purchased by cheese factory manager Frank Butler. The property (pictured above in 1932) was owned by the Butler family for 40 years. The cheese factory burned in 1915; upon its foundations, Butler built a home for his family that is still in use today as the community center for Parkhaven residents. The street that runs through the development is named Oliva Drive in honor of its beginnings.

RANCHES AND FARMS

Between the end of Vineyard Road and Novato Boulevard, the 1,408-acre Redmond/Ryan Ranch was a century-old dairy operation. It had a herd of 207 Holstein milk cows, 59 Guernseys and Jerseys, 65 Holstein heifers, and 4 bulls when it was taken by eminent domain as the site of the new Novato Dam. The Ryan family was paid $155,000 for a large portion of their choice pastureland. Stafford Lake and Dam, completed in 1951, was named in memory of Dr. Charles Stafford, a local veterinarian and president of the North Marin Water District. The 139 acres now host a park, the lake, nature trails, and sporting facilities.

RANCHES AND FARMS

Col. Alexis Rupert Paxton, a native of Philadelphia, Pennsylvania, purchased his property in 1911 and added adjacent parcels in 1915 and 1920. The Paxton orchards produced pears, walnuts, plums, almonds, and grapes and operated from 1925 to 1935. Note the walnut trees along the road leading to the gate at the junction of Hill Road and Diablo Avenue. The tip of the wild oats at the far left foreground points directly at the Regallo house on Center Road. Now a portion of the property is home to Hill Middle School, built in 1955, and the Margaret Todd Senior Center, built in 1992.

RANCHES AND FARMS

In 1954, the members of a civic committee made the decision to build a high school in Novato. A 38-acre parcel of land in the hills off South Novato Boulevard was purchased from Joseph F. Brazil. Construction at the site (seen now in the middle of the picture below) commenced in 1955. When the first students attended in 1957, the high school consisted of the basic classrooms, a library, a cafeteria, and an office building around a quad. The first class to graduate from Novato High School was in 1959 with a total of 89 students.

By 1891, Azorean immigrant Antonio DeBorba owned this tract of land in the vicinity of what is now Redwood Boulevard and Diablo Avenue. DeBorba partnered with Manuel Branco and operated the Black Point Creamery at Deer Island. In 1962, the Novato Fair Shopping Center was constructed on the site, which also was a baseball field in the mid-20th century. The shopping center is anchored by Safeway grocery store and numerous retail shops and restaurants.

RANCHES AND FARMS

RESIDENCES

Hermann Rudolff emigrated from Germany in 1893. He owned the successful Novato French Cheese Factory, which he established in 1898, and eventually became Novato's town judge, a role he served in from 1914 until his death in 1947.

In 1899, he built a stately Romanesque Victorian home on Railroad Avenue across from the cheese factory. The Rudolff home was torn down in 1969 to make way for the new Highway 101 overpass.

Built in 1865, this building housed both the Francis DeLong and Joseph Sweetser families during the height of Rancho Novato's agricultural days (see page 35). It became the home of the Robert H. Trumbull family in 1905 as he supervised the subdivision of the ranch for the Novato Land Company. In the 1950s, the home and surrounding lands were purchased by John Novak, who built a number of individual residences around it. The majestic house has been restored and converted to use as a retreat center for the Opus Dei Society of the Catholic Church.

John and Frances Sweetser built their Italianate Victorian home in 1880 at the end of today's Elm Drive. The home stayed in their family until the late 1930s, when it was purchased by the Pini family. Henry Pini sold the home to Clara Myers and George Schilling in 1945. In 1959, the home was purchased by Harold McCormick, who razed the house and built the Elm Street Apartments in its place. In front of the apartments, two palm trees remain from the Sweetser era.

Stephen Porcella, the local blacksmith, lived in the back of his shop building. When the time came for him to seriously think about taking a bride, he knew he could not bring her home to his simple quarters. He built a house behind the Fashion Shop (see page 15) in 1897 for the sum of $700. After Porcella married Minnie Saunders-Hopkins, they moved into the house, and family members occupied the home until 1977. Today it houses Le Cut of Marin beauty salon.

RESIDENCES

Built in 1892, this home became known as the Carlile House after Charles and Clara Belle Carlile purchased it in 1902. Charles Carlile was a prominent figure in Novato's early days, and the family's home was often the social center for meetings, card games, and musical performances. Many architectural elements that adorned the building, including the gingerbread trim, remain today. It has been restored and renovated and currently serves as the home of the Novato Chamber of Commerce. (On a side note, the home next door was built at the same time as the Carlile House and is a sister or twin home, as they were built as duplicates.)

Now known as the Simmons House, this residence at 900 Sherman Avenue was built in 1906 by the Neilsens, an Ignacio ranching family. At that time, it was widely admired for its impressive detailing, both exterior and interior, and for its elegant furnishings. A butcher named Simmons later occupied the house during his retirement. The house served as office space for the City of Novato staff from 1988 until 2005. It is currently vacant.

Frederick Hamilton settled in Novato in 1904 after moving his family from Kansas. Shortly after arriving, Fred formed a partnership with his brother, James, and opened the Hamilton Brothers General Store (see page 19) at the corner of Grant and Sherman Avenues. In the early 1900s, people generally lived close to their jobs, and Fred built his home at 820 Sherman Avenue, directly behind the store. Today the house is home to Nine Corners: The Center for Balanced Living.

George Washington Oliver was born in Crescent City, California, and moved to Novato in 1893 to manage the California Creamery. He bought the property right across the street from it and built a home at 906 Railroad Avenue. After his early death, his widow, Margie Oliver, moved to San Francisco, but she returned to the house after the earthquake of 1906. She allowed the town's physician, Dr. John Henry Kuser, to use the extra rooms in her home for a hospital, calling it the Novato Sanatorium, which remained active until World War I. The home is now a restored private residence.

While Capt. Leo Hiribarren was operating the Novato House Hotel (see page 13), he built the home at 904 Railroad Avenue (left) in 1906. His descendants still own the home but no longer live there. Antonio DeBorba opened DeBorba's Saloon (see page 73) in 1909. He built the home at 900 Railroad Avenue (right) for its convenience to the rail depot and downtown merchants. DeBorba family members still occupy the home.

Guido Paladini, born in Tuscany, Italy, came to Novato in 1920. He became caretaker of the Durbrow Ranch, which had vineyards and pear and apple orchards. Paladini purchased property at the corner of Wilson Avenue and Vineyard Road, adjacent to his brother Primo's land, in 1938. Built in 1939, his was the first house constructed between Vineyard Road and Novato Boulevard and was surrounded by open fields. The house still stands but is surrounded by other houses. It has been owned by the Daniel Wise family for two generations.

Standing in front of the farmhouse he built in 1893, city pioneer and state assemblyman John Atherton (left) poses with members of his family for this c. 1900 photograph. The house was moved in 1946 to make way for Redwood Highway and again in 2004, when it became the focal point of the Atherton Ranch subdivision. Elements of the home's design were replicated in the roofline and ornamental moldings of the adjacent row house condominiums. The home itself has been converted into office space and now houses Atherton Wealth Management.

When Daniel Hayden purchased the hilltop property in 1891, it was on the western boundary of the Black Point ranch. The Hayden House was completed in the spring of 1892 at 850 Lamont Avenue. Daniel Hayden and his family resided there, and it later became the dental office of Dr. H. Julius Conradt. For many years, it was a popular restaurant known as Maison Marin, then the Moose Lodge, and finally Hilltop Café, which closed in 2008. It is currently vacant.

POINTS OF INTEREST

In the early days, Novato's creeks were navigable, linking the city with the rest of the bay and inland California. This photograph from the 1920s shows the sloop *Crockett* offloading supplies at the Wright and Owens feed mill via the Novato Canal, located near the present Gnoss Field. Dredged in 1923 by mill owner William Q. Wright with engineering help from his son, William Jr., the canal was 100 feet wide and over 2 miles long. Once a waterway and now an airfield, the site remains an important connecting point for the city.

Hamilton Air Force Base was a large part of the Novato economy. Opened as Hamilton Army Air Field in 1935, the base was instrumental in West Coast air defense. In the photograph with the color guard, the main gate that many residents identify with the base can be seen behind them. Hamilton AFB was decommissioned in 1976 and is now a planned mixed-used community. The developers of Hamilton Field reconstructed the new main gate in the Spanish eclectic style to blend with the historic architecture of the base.

(G14-32E-HF) (2-28-35) HEADQUARTERS, HAMILTON FIELD

Building 500 at Hamilton Field was the original headquarters of the army air base and was where the war room was located. The war room was on the second floor; its intricately detailed window can be seen above the entrance door. The room is still used for community meetings. The building has been repurposed and restored and serves as the Novato Art Center, which houses artist studios, the Marin Museum of Contemporary Art, galleries, and a gift store.

Located at the corner of South Novato Boulevard and Center Road, the Cabbage Patch was a huge vegetable garden owned by Italian immigrant Peter Nave. He purchased the land in 1898 and farmed there until he was into his 80s. The rich topsoil that overflowed from Novato Creek made the site an ideal location for growing vegetables. Nave had a small store and fruit and vegetable stand that were a popular stop for locals and travelers passing by on the San Rafael–Petaluma County Road. It is now the site of a gas station at the corner of the Nave Shopping Center.

POINTS OF INTEREST

Henry Hess chose an opportune time to build his lumberyard at the end of Grant Avenue across from the railroad station. In the 1920s, tracts of land were being sold to build homes and businesses as the town was rapidly expanding. The railroad tracks along the property were used to ship in building supplies. Now Novato Builders Supply continues offering lumber and other building supplies.

The Village Inn, originally located at the corner of Redwood Highway and Grant Avenue, was previously known as DeBorba's Stage Station (see page 30). In 1935, Laura Rodoni bought the building and started the Village Inn. When the highway was widened in 1945–1946, the building was moved to the corner of Redwood Highway and Vallejo Avenue, where it was operated by Dave Crandall for 12 years. The building was demolished in 1965 to make way for a used car lot and eventually Grand Auto store, now Big O Tires.

Joe Simontacchi bought this bar in 1951 and operated it for 35 years. The main building was originally a small home located at 7609 Redwood Highway. Joe's X-Road appealed to families and square dancers who used the pavilion behind the bar. The adjacent oak grove once was the setting for annual barbeques hosted by several organizations, including the Novato Fire Department. In the 1960s and 1970s, motorcycle clubs such as the Hell's Angels and racing teams from Sears Point Raceway patronized the bar. Now an office complex named Redwood Crossroads occupies the 2-acre parcel.

During the 1950s, a quarry on Mount Burdell was operating on the site that the Buck Institute now occupies. Richard E. Rush purchased the quarry in 1956 and formed the Marin Rock and Asphalt Company, which expanded the operation. The quarry was closed in 1965. The Buck Institute—the first independent research facility in the United States focused solely on aging and age-related disease—was constructed between 1996 and 1999 on the former mining site. The travertine-clad building was designed by I. M. Pei and is known for its modern lines and light-filled meditative spaces.

Novato Airport was established in 1946 by Paul Binford and Jack Lewis. Both Binford and Lewis had been pilots in World War II, Binford as a flight instructor and Lewis as a P-38 pilot. A runway was graded on a northeast/southwest direction and an aircraft tie-down, auto parking, and a small terminal were built. In 1965, Marin County purchased 40 acres and established Marin County Airport at Gnoss Field, which is half a mile southwest of the original airport. Now 120 acres, it is home base to nearly 300 small aircraft.

The Burdell Mansion was situated on what was originally the 8,877-acre Olompali Rancho, purchased by James Black in the 1850s. In 1911, a wood-frame home was replaced with a 26-room stucco mansion encasing a 19th-century (and possibly earlier) adobe house within its walls. After serving as a retreat center and private club, it was occupied in the late 1960s by a hippie commune. The mansion burned down in 1969. Today the property is part of the California State Park System and is called Olompali State Park. The bases of the columns of the 1911 mansion can be seen to the lower left of the outbuilding that now occupies the site.

COMMUNITY LIFE

The Novato Colts were a semipro baseball team. This photograph was taken about 1915. Bill Gnoss became the team's manager and center fielder. Babe Silva, businessman and city council member, was recruited by the St. Louis Browns. The man in the white shirt at center is E. R. Samuels, the first manager of the Colts. Prior to the 1920s, the ball field was between Reichert Avenue and Scott Street.

Zunino Shoe Repair, one of Novato's oldest businesses, has been in the same family and celebrates its 100th anniversary in 2010. The 1913 photograph shows Angelo at work on a sheet finishing machine. The original location was near the train depot; however, when the rent was raised from $7.50 to $7.65 a month, Angelo moved his shop to 928 Grant Avenue and turned the business over to his son Leo, who owned the shop for 54 years. The business, still in operation today at 904 Grant Avenue, is owned by Angelo's grandson Ernie Zunino and his wife, who still use equipment that his grandfather and father used. (Then image courtesy of the Zunino family.)

The 1964 photograph is of barbers Nick Delporie (left) and Bob Comanduran (right), and seated is Terry Kellogg. The recent photograph is of Bob (standing) and Terry 45 years later (Nick passed away in 2006). Bob opened his barbershop in 1959, and it is now one of the longest continuously operating barbershops in Novato, located at 1553 South Novato Boulevard. Terry worked for Bob from 1964 to 1978 and has had his own barbershop for 25 years at 816 Grant Avenue.

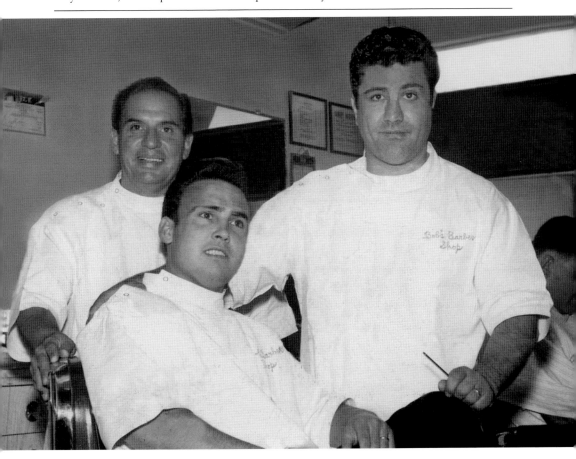

Arriving in Novato in 1922, Guglielmo and Natalina Torassa worked at a newly opened bakery on Grant Avenue. They eventually purchased full ownership of it, and in 1937, they built a residential/commercial building next door at 812 Grant, where they worked and lived until their deaths in the mid-1950s. Now the building has been remodeled for use as a jewelry store. At the time of the most recent remodel, the bakery ovens were found in the walls of the back room and removed.

Anthony ("Tony") DeBorba opened his bar in 1909 as an alternative to working on his father's Deer Island dairy. The family owns and operates the bar to this day. There was an interruption in operation during Prohibition years, during which it was used as a pool hall. As seen in the comparison of the *c.* 1950 photograph, much has remained the same at the saloon.

The Novato Senior Citizens Club is a nonprofit organization sponsored by the City of Novato Parks, Recreation, and Community Services Department. All activities now take place at the Margaret Todd Senior Center. The club has been in existence since 1964 and provides social and recreational opportunities for its membership. The club has many events with a long tradition; shown here is the annual Hawaiian Luau Dinner in 1968 and in 2008. (Both images courtesy of the Novato Senior Citizens Club.)

COMMUNITY LIFE

Founded in 1934, the Novato Garden Club marked its 75th anniversary in 2009, and past presidents (above) were honored during the celebration. Throughout its history, the club members have worked on many community beautification projects—from street-side civic plantings to school landscaping—for which it raises money through plant sales and annual fairs. (Now image courtesy of the Novato Garden Club.)

The Novato 4-H Club was founded in 1927 by Gertrude Lane and was open to youngsters between the ages of 10 and 21. In the early years, the club had an active drum corps that participated in many area parades. Novato 4-H-ers had a variety of agricultural, livestock, and home economics projects over the years and excelled at the county, state, and national levels. The current Indian Valley 4-H Club was formed in 2006 by Toni Shroyer and Erica Hoytt. Poultry and arts and crafts are popular projects with these current 4-H-ers.

In 1942, the Novato Horsemen Club was founded by a group of riding enthusiasts at the home of Mrs. Wayne Tharpe. The ever-growing group built their first clubhouse and riding arena three years later on property purchased from the Bugeia brothers. Through the years, the same site has seen many improvements reflecting the changing interests of the membership. Today the club boasts a diverse membership in excess of 400 individuals and remains active in the community. (Then image courtesy of the Novato Horsemen Club.)

The IDESI Hall at 901 Sweetser Avenue was built in 1908 by the association Irmandade do Divino Espirito Santo Independente or IDESI. Its purpose was to celebrate the annual Holy Ghost Festa and to provide a way to keep traditions alive for Novato's Portuguese immigrants. An adjoining dance hall was added in 1937. A new bar and snack bar were built in 1988. On April 23, 1988, the IDESI Hall became a historic landmark. Today it continues to be a meeting place for Novato's and neighboring Portuguese communities where family and friends can socialize.

Novato's Portuguese community celebrates the Holy Ghost Festa the Sunday before Pentecost. The celebration begins with a parade from the IDESI Hall to Our Lady of Loretto Catholic Church. At the mass, the queen for Novato is crowned. The parade marches back to the IDESI Hall for a traditional meal of *sopas e carne*. In the evening, a dance is held, where many join in to perform the *chamarita*, an Azorean folk dance. In the 1929 photograph, Queen Tessie Mendoza Brazil is shown with her attendants Mary Soares (left) and Emily Cardoza (right). Shown in the 2008 photograph is Queen Mary R. Stompe with her attendants Amber Simonetti (left) and Elizabeth Murphy (right). (Then image courtesy of IDESI, now image courtesy of Mary Wilkinson.)

The Marin County Fair and Harvest Festival was held in Novato in the 1920s. The photograph below shows the horticultural exhibit at the second annual event, held in 1926 at what is now Atherton Ranch. Featured among the usual fair attractions were the best produce and agricultural products from the family farms and ranches in the area.

Continuing the tradition, the Novato Farmer's Market, held every Tuesday on Grant Avenue during the summer, is a place where local farmers, musicians, artists, and community members gather to enjoy the beauty of northern Marin and to buy fresh, locally grown food.

The Renaissance Pleasure Faire was inspired and operated by the Patterson family for over 30 years and annually drew thousands of visitors to the Black Point area of Novato. It was a reenactment of Merrie Olde England in the Renaissance period, Shakespeare's time. There were five open-air stages, winding lanes with merchants, musicians, singers, parades and puppetry, jousting, archery, fencing, and hearty food and drink. Part of the land is now the site of Stonetree golf course and home sites, and the remaining portion is an open-space preserve. (Then image courtesy of Ron Vela.)

In the early years of the 20th century, everyone looked forward to the Fourth of July parade and barbecue. Following the parade, there were footraces and a baseball game, concluding the day with a horse race. In the photograph taken in 1913, the Simonds family rides in their decorated horse-drawn wagon. Today the Fourth of July parade is a highlight of the year, with thousands of spectators and many participants. The parade follows Grant Avenue from Reichert Avenue to Seventh Street. In the 2008 photograph, the Novato Historical Guild's float depicts the early pioneers of Novato.

CIVIC LIFE

The present railroad depot was built in 1917. It was constructed on the site after the former depot burned. The freight depot to the left of the passenger depot partially burned in the 1990s and was torn down in 2008 to make way for redevelopment. It is hoped that the currently vacant depot will be restored.

The arrival of the Northwestern Pacific Railroad in 1879 changed the character and location of Novato; its first downtown was near Novato Creek on South Novato Boulevard. The first train station was constructed in 1879, and the new downtown built up around it. The first station deteriorated rapidly and was replaced in 1903 by a more substantial structure on the same site. The original railroad depot was moved to its present site on Reichert Avenue behind the Druids Hall, where it is maintained by members of the Druids.

The Black Point drawbridge was built to cross the Petaluma Creek for the Napa Marin Railroad in the 1880s. This branch was built off the main line in Ignacio and went to Sonoma and Glen Ellen. Northwest Pacific Railroad later used this line for freight trains only. Land for the Black Point Highway Bridge was donated in 1922 by Antonio DeBorba. Currently the Black Point Highway Bridge is part of Highway 37.

The Novato Fire District was formed in 1926 and encompassed 75 square miles. The first station was constructed in 1930 at the Grant Avenue and Redwood Highway intersection. It was remodeled extensively in the 1950s and demolished in the early 1990s after sustaining damage in the 1989 earthquake. The station that now serves downtown, Station 1, was opening on September 10, 1988, and is located on Redwood Boulevard a half-mile south of the original location. There are now five stations that serve the district.

The Hamilton Field Firehouse was built in 1934. Although the first official firehouse on the base, another was constructed adjacent to the hangars and runways. The Novato Historical Guild and the City of Novato have renovated the building, which will open as the Hamilton Field History Museum in May 2010.

The first Catholic church in Novato was a mission of St. Vincent's in Petaluma. In 1892, Our Lady of Loretto was officially declared a Catholic parish, and the lovely Victorian wood-frame church was constructed on South Novato Boulevard on a knoll. The wood-frame structure burned to the ground in 1936, and another church was built on Grant Avenue (see page 32). Growth of the church in the 1950s led to the construction of the present church, located on Novato Boulevard a few miles north of the 1892 site, which the parish first occupied in 1963.

Catholic Church, Novato, Cal.

Captured in this rare 1880s lithograph, Pioneer Memorial Cemetery is the resting place for many city pioneers, including the Atherton and Sweetser families. Several of the pines circling the base of the knoll still stand, as do the prominent spires, less visible amid the broad oaks and plantings that cover the cemetery knoll. Plans during the 1960s to remove the cemetery, at that time declared abandoned, galvanized a grassroots effort to help preserve it led by city historians Margaret Coady and Wilfred Lieb. After nearly a decade, the city was convinced to restore the landmark. Pioneer Cemetery remains a monument to the men and women who helped found Novato and to the generation who fought to preserve their memory.

From 1917 until the 1950s, the post office was located on Grant Avenue next to the Novato Bank (see page 20). Theodora ("Theda") Bugeia (shown here) got a job delivering the mail when a Mr. Ross, the town mailman, went into the army during World War I. Bugeia used a horse and buggy, and her route included 125 mailboxes. When Bugeia retired in 1947, her route included 465 mailboxes. Now the Novato Post Office is in the Nave Shopping Center on South Novato Boulevard and Center Road.

Many one-room schoolhouses were found in the assorted communities in and around the town of Novato. Black Point School, at 433 School Road, began in 1896 with 14 boys and 9 girls. The school clerk was James Smith. The school operated until the late 1940s and is now a private residence.

The Novato Community House, built in 1922, is located at the corner of Machin Street and DeLong Avenue. The project was spearheaded by several prominent individuals but was built through the dedication and hard work of the entire community. The community house was used by church groups and fraternal organizations, as a library, and for school graduations, wedding receptions, civic meetings, dances, theater productions, recitals, and many other events. This well-loved building was utilized until April 2005, when it was deemed unsafe and closed to the public. It now awaits restoration.

CIVIC LIFE

Although located on two earlier sites, the Novato branch of the Marin County Library opened on August 21, 1927, upstairs in the community house. The first librarian was Margaret Clark. It moved to a few other locations in town as it grew, and on April 15, 1971, the Novato regional branch opened in a new 10,300-square-foot building at 1720 Novato Boulevard, where it continues to serve the people of Novato. On June 5, 2004, a South Novato branch opened in Hangar 6 at Hamilton Landing.

When Novato was incorporated in 1960, city officials found a ready-made city hall. It was the former Presbyterian church, which was built in 1896. The old white church was painted dark red with white trim and in 1963 began to be used as Novato's city hall. Recent renovation of the city hall included building a new foundation and reinforcing it. City council meetings will be held there with seating for 120. It will also serve as a public venue for events such as receptions, banquets, and small performances. Today the building at 901 Sherman Avenue is the most photographed of Marin's city halls and is a symbol of Novato.

The Postmaster's House was built around 1850 and was originally located on South Novato Boulevard, west of Yukon Way. The earliest occupant was Henry Jones, who began Novato's postal service in 1856. In 1972, then-owner Fabian Bobo agreed to give the house to the City of Novato if they would move it so he could build apartments. The city accepted the offer, and the house was towed up Redwood Boulevard to its present site at 815 DeLong Avenue. The renovated house is now the home of the Novato History Museum and Archives.

www.arcadiapublishing.com

Discover books about the town where you grew up, the cities where your friends and families live, the town where your parents met, or even that retirement spot you've been dreaming about. Our Web site provides history lovers with exclusive deals, advanced notification about new titles, e-mail alerts of author events, and much more.

MADE IN THE USA

Arcadia Publishing, the leading local history publisher in the United States, is committed to making history accessible and meaningful through publishing books that celebrate and preserve the heritage of America's people and places. Consistent with our mission to preserve history on a local level, this book was printed in South Carolina on American-made paper and manufactured entirely in the United States.

This book carries the accredited Forest Stewardship Council (FSC) label and is printed on 100 percent FSC-certified paper. Products carrying the FSC label are independently certified to assure consumers that they come from forests that are managed to meet the social, economic, and ecological needs of present and future generations.

FSC
Mixed Sources
Product group from well-managed forests and other controlled sources

Cert no. SW-COC-001530
www.fsc.org
© 1996 Forest Stewardship Council

Find Your Place in History.